The Conquerors of Evil

Marvin Mims Sr. and Hazen Desmond Walker

The Conquerors of Evil

This is the story of real-life superheroes who come to the rescue of friends, family, and community.

Published in the United States by Marvin Mims Sr. and Hazen Desmond Walker
Memphis, TN

Boldtn04@yahoo.com and Hazendesmond@gmail.com

Contributing editor Jairus Prince Winfrey
zpinupe@gmail.com

Contributing editor Takenya Anica Mims
authortakenyamims@gmail.com

Contributing editor LaJOYce Harris

Illustrated by Creative Next
thecreativenext@gmail.com

Formatted by Nonon Tech & Design

Marvin Mims Sr. and Hazen Desmond Walker, Co-Authors | Mims Sr., Marvin, Editor

United States | Family | African-American Families

ISBN: 979-8-218-52062-5 (Paperback)
ISBN: 979-8-218-52063-2 (Hardback)

Cover designed by Nonon Tech & Design and Hazen Desmond Walker

Dedication

In memory of Hazen's late great-grandmothers, Mrs. John Ella Bachus and Mrs. Tereather Addie Mims, this book is dedicated to Anita Mims, Angela Mims, Takenya Mims, and Tracy Ann Walker. Along with Hazen's cousins Frederick Patterson and Kendrick Patterson, and Hazen's father Joshua Walker.

INTRODUCTION

Welcome to *The Conquerors of Evil*—a magical journey where everyday heroes face the greatest challenges and emerge victorious! In this enchanting book, we dive into the lives of real-life superheroes who use their extraordinary gifts to conquer doubt, depression, hatred, and discouragement. These heroes aren't just found in comic books or movies; they are around us every day, showing incredible courage, wisdom, kindness, and healing.

Within these pages, you'll discover how these amazing individuals tap into their inner strength and supernatural powers to overcome obstacles and make the world a better place. But here's the secret: you have the power of a superhero inside you too!

The Conquerors of Evil is here to inspire you to find your own heroic qualities and recognize them in those around you. As you read, you'll see how simple acts of kindness and bravery can shine brightly, even in the darkest times. This book will encourage you to be a beacon of hope and to lend a helping hand to others who need it.

So, gear up and get ready! The adventure is just beginning, and it's time for you to step into your superhero shoes. With every page, you'll learn how to rescue someone in need, making the world a more wonderful place with your very own superpowers. Remember, you are a superhero—go out there and make a difference!

CHAPTER 1
The Conquerors of Evil
CONQUERING DOUBT

CHAPTER 2

The Conquerors of Evil

CONQUERING DEPRESSION

CHAPTER 3
The Conquerors of Evil
CONQUERING HATRED

CHAPTER 4
The Conquerors of Evil
CONQUERING DISCOURAGEMENT

Color Your Superheroes